A Mother's Poems

Thelma Edwards

Thelma Edwards

Published by:
Anointed Words Publishing Co.

All Rights Reserved. No part of this book may be used or
reproduced in any manner whatsoever without the expressed
written permission of the author. Address all inquiries to:
2244 Shawnee Rd, #109
Lima, OH 45805
Email: awpubco@gmail.com
www.awpubco.com

ISBN: 978-0-9977397-6-3
Printed in the United States of America

Contents

A Mother's Poems

A Mother's Poems

Dedication

I dedicate this book to God, my Father, to Jesus my Savior and Friend, and to the precious Holy Spirit who teaches me and gives me peace.

I dedicate this book to pastors, Ronald and Carol Fails and Grace World Wide Ministries. Also, to our family of God. We love to pray for each other.

I dedicate this book to my mother, Sarah M. Lusk for her unwavering love of God, and to my dad, Carl E. Lusk for the unspoken love shown in his eyes.

I also dedicate this book to my children whose pure love has blessed every day of my life.

Acknowledgment

I would like to acknowledge Dr. Leah McCray, owner of Anointed Words Publishing, for her encouragement and help in fulfilling my lifelong dream of seeing this book in print. What a joy to share the love of God!

I would also like to thank my daughter Nina Gondola and my son and daughter John and Leslie Martin for typing the pages. I thank God for your love and caring.

Thank you too, my precious granddaughter, April Marie Dean, for the cover designs you sent. I chose the bouquet of flowers, because that's what we are to God. Fantastic beauty.

Introduction

I asked my mother questions about everything. She said, "If you have a problem and I can't fix it, just talk to Jesus. Ask Him. I was six years old. He always answered.

I'm ninety one years old now. My life has been filled with trials and tests of every kind. But Jesus is still my safe haven. I go to Him knowing that in His name alone, I overcome.

There is a sweetness of His Holy Spirit that lives inside of us, when we really know Him. There is a lonely heart hunger when we don't.

It's so easy to know Him. Just tell Him you're tired of trying to make it alone, and ask Him to take your life and change it. He will, and you'll know, because of the peace He gives.

I love you all so very much, my sisters and brothers in Christ. No wonder Jesus said, "Love your neighbor as yourself."

The Family That Prays Together

Who can describe Earth's family?
Our souls are kin to each other.
We laugh, and we cry, but always
get by, as long as we pray
together.

When one is hurt, love rallies
'round in spite of the situation.
We sometimes scold, but always
help, regardless of trepidation.

A family will reward with praise
Every success we achieve.
And God above pours out His love
with each blessing that we
receive.

God's family is a pattern
for our families here below.
We are a part of the heart of God.
No wonder we love Him so.

Follow Christ Each Day

Jesus is the only name
We can call on to be saved,
And over all who trust in Him,
His banner will be waved.

The way to know Him is easy.
Be honest with Him and pray.
Ask Him to come into your heart,
And to wash your sins away.

Life is just an experiment,
One step forward, two steps back.
Unless you listen to the Lord,
Who'll keep you right on track.

All the riches you'll ever need
Are not of the earthly kind.
Study the Scriptures every day.
His Word brings us peace of
mind.

Do you praise God when you're
tested?

When you're living through the
pain?
You have to be refined by fire,
Eternity with God to attain.

Alone with God

Sometimes I need a quiet place
Where I can just slip away,
And talk to God to find release
From all the cares of the day.

And oh the blessings Jesus sends
When I call upon His name.
The Holy Spirit fills my soul.
I never will be the same.

Marriage

It takes a lot of caring,
A lot of smiles and sharing.
It takes an equal pairing
Of happiness and tears.

To make a life together
With side by side endeavor,
In spite of storms to weather,
God will guide us through the
years.

All we have to do is pray,
Walk in His footsteps all the way,
Listen to what He has to say,
And trust in Him. He hears.

It just takes faith, believing,
With giving and receiving,
A worthwhile life achieving,
Trusting God, there are no fears.

Dialogue

"Father God, please give me good
health."
"Take care of the body I gave
you."

"Father God, please give me more
strength."
"You had it the minute I made
you."

"Father God, it's wisdom I need."
"Just a mustard seed's worth will
do you."

"Father God, I don't understand."
"My words are the wisdom to
guide you."

"Father God, what if I stray?"
"You can't if my Spirit's inside
you."

We Appreciate our Pastor

Thank you, God, for the
Shepherd
You have sent to guide our way.
He teaches us your Holy Word,
Lest we should be led astray.

Bless him Jesus, anoint him.
Give him wisdom, strength and
care,
And let us undergird him,
When we call on You in prayer.

Communication

When a child of God
Meets a child of God,
We recognize His love

And we share His praise
All of our days,
For blessings from above.

Blessings

Love is a warm glow
Where tears might have been.
Joy is like sunshine,
Or rainbows within.

Trust is a waiting
Prayer is our part.
Peace is communion
With God in the heart.

Jesus

Oh, God, my Savior, I'm thankful
Lord, that your Spirit lives inside.
I call upon your precious name,
And know that you abide.

You're here to answer every
prayer. I trust your Holy Word.
So freely I just come to you,
And know that you have heard.

Cast All Your Care Upon Him

Be still my soul and patiently
wait.
The Lord you love will not be late.
He made the mountains. He
formed the hills.
He knows about your monthly
bills.

Assurance

When you meet the Savior
And know His perfect will,
When He pours out joy and
peace, your empty heart to fill,

Then you know the reason
Your heart has searched for
years,
Looking for the Son of God,
Who casts out all your fears.

His Message

God will teach you what to say,
To be His witness day by day.
Read His Words, watch and pray.
Simply trust Him, come what
may.

To Another Child of God

Once in a while I meet someone,
A friend so precious and dear.
I pray God's awesome presence
Will always be lingering near,

To keep you in His perfect peace,
In His loving sheltering care,
To let you know His Holy Word
Assured that He is there.

Life is a Gift from God

Like a pebble tossed in a pond,
Concentric circles move on and
on.

How transient this life is!
I'm aware.
My heart touches the circles I
share.

Faith

Because He died on Calvary's
tree,
The gift of God to ransom me,
Because He hears my trembling
prayer,
And when I cry, He's always
there,
And always lifts my searching
soul,
Ever higher toward its' goal
-- I trust in God.

Love

Love is understanding each
other's vulnerabilities,
As well as our capabilities,
Then letting ourselves know
That we can share -- at the heart
level.

Reality

Do I love you, God, with all my
heart?
Do I love you with all my soul?
Do I love my neighbor as myself?
Am I living my Savior's goal?

Do I honor my earthly mother?
Do I honor my father too?
Do I lie or whisper to others
As I've been forbidden to do?

Thank you, God, that you show
me myself,
Directing my path day by day,
And thank you God for giving me
peace
In a world that has gone astray.

My Prayer

What kind of lesson do you want
me to learn,
Lord, from you today?
My heart reaches out to so many
I love.
Teach me what to say.

Introspect

Sometimes we meet others and
are not aware of how much all
our lives will touch.

We talk, and we smile, and all of
the while fail to recognize friends
as such.

Then as time passes by, we smile,
and we sigh on the daily path of
our living.

We learn to rejoice when others
rejoice and welcome the loving
and giving.

Until we can feel what the other
man feels and can share in his
joy and his pain,

Thelma Edwards

We never can know the depth of
ourselves, how much happiness
we can contain.

Come Unto Me

When you are hurting,
And can't find the anwers,
When you need comfort
For pain you can't share,

When your heart travels
A maze of confusion,
When you need someone
To lovingly care,

When every day brings the
Same endless problems,
When walking in circles
Is grossly unfair,

When life seems to laugh,
And to mock all your efforts,
When no one is able
To ease your despair,

Come unto me. I am the source of
compassion.

Come unto me. I give release from
your cares.
Come unto me. I'll give you peace
everlasting.
Come unto me. I'll answer your
prayers.

John 14:6 (King James Bible)

My Friend

You've been a good friend.
Let's not lose touch.
For as time passes,
Friends mean so much.

Friends are constant, through
Joy or through pain,
They lift up our hearts
Again and again.

We Are Never Alone

For every burden that we bear,
For every sorrow, every care,
For every joy and every pain,
For every loss and every gain,
Christ's love surrounds us every
day.
His gentle presence guides our
way.

A Testimony of Praise

When a child of God starts
singing,
The angels sing along,
And God above shares His love,
Anointing every song.

Trust

Whether it brings joy,
Or whether it brings sorrow,
I know that my God
Holds my tomorrow.

In His Care

Whenever I'm in a hurry,
And I have too much to do,
I just stop and breathe a prayer
To the One who sees me through.

The day always goes much
smoother.
Frustrations just melt away,
And God puts a song in my heart,
Because I took time to pray.

Innocence

Oh, the love we take for granted
When we're young and free of
care,
Children trust in innate
goodness,
Finding laughter everywhere.

In His Presence Daily

Thank you, God, for the precious
friends who crossed my path
today.
You pour your loving blessings
out in such an awesome way.

Guide me, Lord, in your Holy
Will.
Teach me to reconcile
Those who do not know You,
To be, "My Father's Child."

Thank You, God

When I think about you, Jesus,
And what you did for me,
Leaving, "Heaven's Glory,"
To die, to set me free.

I thank you, precious Savior.
My heart cries out to you.
Teach me Lord, your, 'Holy Will,'
Oh, let my heart be true.

For mistakes I seem to make,
Forgive me, Lord, I pray,
Let them all be stepping stones
To keep me in your way.

My spirit is so willing,
But, flesh is sometimes weak.
Let me keep my trust in you,
And listen when you speak.

I prayed just to be closer.

I felt I needed more.
You sent your Holy Spirit.
It filled me to the core.

At first, I felt so empty.
I had lived with so much pain,
That when you filled my heart
with joy,
My peace was like fresh rain.

It washed away all my fears,
And all that came between
My soul and your, "Holy Will,"
With beauty, fresh and clean,
And now, I've come to understand
That with your awesome love,
You're using every choice I make
To lead me home above.

Reconciliation

My life was filled with emptiness,
A day after day lonely game.
I know I grieved the heart of God,
But He loved me just the same.

Father, I met your Holy Son,
And He accepted me.
In spite of all that I had done,
He redeemed me and set me free.

My Savior gave me brand new
eyes.
I see beauty everywhere.
He filled my soul with calm and
peace,
And His yearning love to share.

He is the vine that gives me life.
I am one of His branches,
And when I look at you, I see
myself,

In other circumstances.

I too was searching for the truth.
I wondered, "Why was I born?"
The world seemed full of ugliness,
And with grief and anguish torn.

My heart had nowhere else to go.
I asked Jesus, "Are you real?"
And He in loving kindness came,
Redeemed me and set His seal.

Now I share the Gospel of Christ,
And His death on Calvary,
And how our Father raised Him
up
To offer eternity.

But oh, the power of His Blood,
The Blood that was shed for me,
He was the only sacrifice
That could ever set me free.

Holy Spirit, with your presence,
Let me win others today.
Let me tell the story again.
Help me show others the way.

Thoughts

Here I am in the mall
Watching people walk by,
Some are smiling at friends.
Some are alone, as I.

Each has his own purpose,
Living life day by day.
God watches over us all.
How many think to pray?

The Answer

God can take away your
emptiness,
Your inner sense of loneliness,
And fill your soul with
peacefulness
Through Jesus Christ --
His Son

Mothers and Daughters are Special

When a mother looks into the
eyes
Of her small precious baby girl,
She is overwhelmed with love and
joy
As she gently touches a curl.

Then as she finds the soft little
hand,
She presses a finger inside,
And is amazed at the clutching
strength.
Her heartstrings forever are tied.

When God pours out
unquenchable love
Into the heart of that mother,
He knows it will grow and be
passed on
From one child to another.

Mothers pray, "Oh God, take care
of her,
I can't do this all alone."
You have loaned her to me for
awhile,
But I know that she is your own.

Lord, just as my mother taught
me to trust,
And to talk to you each day,
I'll teach this child, that whatever
comes,
You'll answer her prayers when
she prays.

Help me to teach her the right
from the wrong,
And I'll teach her to try, try again.
I'll show her how very much that
she's loved,
Then I'll tell her, "I know that you
can."

A mother always kisses small
hurts.
She gives hugs whether they're
needed.
A child comes to us like we go to
God,

Knowing her wants will be
heeded.
Little girls love to play with their
dolls.
They mother their 'children' with
care,
Imitating their own mother's love.
There is nothing that can
compare.

And we try to instill a sense of
worth
That nothing can ever destroy,
But only Christ can open a heart
To fill it with purpose and joy.

When she grows up and has her
own home,
With a husband and child to love,
The circle starts all over again.
It's God's plan from heaven
above.

Healing

God, my Father, sent His Son,
To cleanse my heart and soul.
Now I'm filled with joy and peace.
Heaven is my goal.

Jesus, help me share your love
In helpful, caring ways.
Make my life a guiding light,
Offering up praise.

Spring Rain

The grass is green.
The sky is blue.
The air is clean,
All rainwashed new.

Attitudes

Every day I sow a seed
With every word I speak,
Whether it's anger filled,
Or whether it is meek.

I hear a voice deep inside,
For this child too, I died.
Share the love I gave to you.
My arms are still open wide.

I will watch the words I speak,
They could cause joy or pain.
I will be God's witness.
There are souls to lose or gain.

Deja' Vu

I see a little blond haired boy
Playing with his brother.
They're having lots and lots of fun
Chasing one another.

Is their mother teaching them
The old, old sweet story,
How Jesus died to save us all,
Leaving "Heaven's Glory?"

Their innocent childhood joy
Causes me to pray,
"Lead and guide, protect them,
Lord,"
Each and every day.

How children's voices steal my
heart.
I still can hear my own,
Across the miles, across the
years,
Each time they telephone,

And I reflect on bygone days,
Memories are sweet;
Recalling sounds of laughter
In every child I meet.

Today

Everything is wet and gray
This rainy, icy, gloomy day,
And I will feel a little blue
Until the sun comes shining
through.

They say that dark days have to
come
Before the winter season's done,
And we go through a testing time
Until the summer's balmy clime.

But come what may, I always
pray,
For God has my life in His hands,
And I stand steadfast in the love
Of a Savior who understands.

Liberty

Why was I afraid to show
My inside self to you?
Was it because I might be hurt
By things you'd say or do?

My soul was like a timid child,
I'd never let you see.
I'd never let you have a glimpse
Of the person who was me.

But oh, the love that Jesus gave
When He redeemed my soul.
It grows and grows and overflows
Since He has made me whole,

And now I'm not afraid to say
Just what He's done for me,
And He will do the same for you,
His love will set you free.

Seasons of Life

Icy frost pictures on windows in
winter
Show tropical ferns of a time long
ago.
They glisten in sunshine with
rare pristine beauty,
A legacy only our God could
bestow.

When Springtime comes with all
of its' new life,
When all of the brown earth turns
soft green again,
We think about God and how He
has promised
A new life through Christ, the
renewing of man.

When soft summer showers cool
hot summer days,
Or dark storm clouds pelt down
cold rain,

The earth keeps renewing itself in
His care,
And rainbows remind us, our life
He'll sustain.

Then warm autumn nights with
glorious sunsets
Give place to the quiet of bright
winter days,
And all of creation takes time for
resting,
For reconsecration and worship
and praise.

God Understands

Oh God, I'm in the process
Of growing more like you,
And in my tests and trials,
I know you'll see me through.

You said your strength was
enough,
If I would trust and pray,
But I am sad and afraid.
I slipped right back today.

Lord, will you forgive my sin?
I'm so alone and lost.
Help me, Lord, to make amends
No matter what the cost.

My heart is filled with anguish.
Will you still hear my prayer?
Can I really live for you?
I know that you are there.

Why did I choose to do it?

My life is empty now.
Fill my heart again with love,
As at your feet, I bow.

I asked my Lord and Savior,
"Do you still care for me?"
"Help me turn my life around,
Your child I want to be."

"My strength is made perfect in
weakness,"
Is what He said to me,
And then He touched my broken
heart,
And said, He died for me.

Bring your thoughts under
control.
My Spirit is your guide.
Study my words every day.
You'll have my joy inside.

Living a life for Jesus?
Get up each time you fall.
The way may not be easy.
Just keep on standing tall.

Remember, love your neighbor.
He has a load of care.

Act like Christ and be a friend,
And let him know you're there.

With every test that we go
through,
He brings us closer still,
Teaching us and leading us
Into His holy will.

Now I know just what to do.
I'll live life day by day.
Trusting in my Savior's love,
And from Him, I'll not stray.

Opportunity

For every door that closes
Another opens wide.
God knows our inner feelings,
And He will surely guide.

No matter what each day brings,
We never are alone.
He's with us every step we take,
When we become His own.

Trusting Jesus? Oh the joy
To know we're in His care.
Just to shelter in His love,
Assured that He is there.

The Family of God

Oh, how sweet to fellowship
With those who love the Lord,
To worship and to praise Him,
And share His Holy Word.

Appreciation

My life has changed
Since Christ saved me,
And now I know
Serenity.

A perfect world
He made for me.
I'll praise His Name
Eternally.

Observation/Then Prayer

Father, I look out at the world
From this quiet place inside.
I see the hurt and feel the pain
That everyone tries to hide.

My Personal Praise

I feel a quiet peacefulness
As the world goes rushing by,
And I tell anyone who's sad,
That Christ is the reason why.

Musing at the Beauty Shop

I'm musing under a dryer
Just contemplating life.
The world is filled with confusion,
Bewilderment and strife.

Each succeeding generation
Walks where others have trod.
Every soul has this lesson to
learn.
The only answer -- God.

Praise to God at Daybreak

I awoke this morning while
The earth was still at rest,
And in the quiet dawning
I knew that I was blessed.

The freshness of the morning
Brought healing to my soul.
I thought about my Savior,
And how He'd made me whole.

What an all compassing love
My Father had for me,
To send His Son to die for me,
There on Calvary.

With His Spirit guiding me,
My life has grown so sweet.
I tell the wondrous story
To everyone I meet.

Life

It's not about money.
It's not about loss.
It's not about having
The world and its' gloss.

It's not about whether
You're short or you're tall,
Or if you have wisdom,
Or no sense at all.

It's not about travel
Or staying at home,
Or whether you're anchored,
Or whether you roam.

It's not about whether
You're happy or sad,
Or if the sun's shining,
Or weather is bad.

It's not about most things
We all think about,
Or if we can make it,

Or if we have doubt.

But it's about trusting,
And it's about love.
It's all about Jesus
In heaven above.

Salvation

Holy Spirit, lift my soul
To higher realms with thee.
Teach my heart the grandeur of
God's simplicity.

I love to tell the story
About our Savior's love,
How He left heaven's glory,
His wondrous home above,

Just to give rebellious man
A chance to be redeemed,
Sin had separated us
With no way back, it seemed.

But our heavenly Father
In wisdom had a plan.
He'd provide the sacrifice,
And let us choose again,

And if we'd choose to serve Him,
Then He would set us free,

Free to go and live for Him
Throughout eternity.

Choose the Son of God today.
Ask Him to be your guide.
He'll give you a loving heart
With peace and joy inside.

Discipleship

God will teach you what to say
To be His witness day by day.
Simply trust Him come what
may.
Trust Jesus Christ, God's Son.

Then use your heart filled with
love
To show the wellsprings from
above,
And humbly teach His awesome
love,
Until your work is done.

Reach Out to Someone

The love of God is so precious.
It comes back when we give it
away;
It brings us the richest blessings
Each day, after day, after day.

Our Example

"Father forgive them," my Savior
cried,
"They know not what they do,"
And with Holy love, He bled and
died,
Forgiving me -- and you.

When we come to Christ in
humble faith,
We know we are His own.
He changes our hearts with love
and peace
Such as we have never known.

When the Holy Spirit enters in,
Our tests will be the same.
But Jesus overcame them all
By the power of His name.

No matter what Satan tries to do,
I will hold fast today.
Since Christ saved me, he wants
me to show

Some other soul the way.

I have a great commission from
God.
He wants me to forgive
Those who are hurtful and lost in
sin,
Some will find Christ and live.

For God's love is beauty
And God's love is sweet,
And we have to share it
With each soul we meet.

Standing Fast

When Satan tries to stop you
In everything you do,
Remember, Christ encountered
The same things we go through.

God always has the answers
When we let Him guide each day.
All we have to do is trust Him,
And He will make a way.

Smile

An infectious grin
Will go a long way
To giving someone
A happier day.

Ask Yourself

Would Jesus say what I just said?
Would He do what I've just done?
Is this the heart of my Savior?
Is this how souls are won?

Where Are You Going?

The time it takes from here to
there
Depends on where you're going,
Or you could sidetrack all around
And end up never knowing.

You have to have a place to start
And have a destination,
Or you will never make it there,
With all your hesitation.

So make a choice for Jesus
Christ,
Or for Satan's living death,
But know that you were made in
heaven
With our Father's "Holy Breath."

Our life is a living journey
That we're all traveling through,
And when we choose life with
Jesus,
Then we're choosing Heaven too.

Invitation

Are you acquainted with God's
own Son?
Has your life been changed
through and through?
Have you prayed for His Holy
Spirit?
There's much more in store then,
for you.

When the Holy Spirit falls on you
With a love far too much to hold,
You have to share it with
everyone.
He enables you to be bold.

Trusting God is the way to find
joy,
So ask Him for guidance each
day.
He will comfort and take care of
you,
And help you show others the
way.

What do you know about Jesus
Christ?
Have you asked Him to save your
soul?
Are you tired of Satan's awful
strife?
Do you want to make Him your
goal?

Eternity and God's endless love,
Or time everlasting with shame,
This is the question to ask
yourself,
There'll be nobody else to blame.

God Is Real

Every test that we go through
Is a blessing in disguise,
Watched in love by God above
With His Spirit there to guide.

He wants us to be ready
To enter "Heaven's Gate."
Why not give your heart to Him,
Before it is too late?

A Mother's Love

A mother's love is like a prism
With God's Holy light shining
through,
To teach her children the colors
of truth
In all that they say or do.

Love teaches patience, quiet and
calm,
How to wait and to understand.
Love is kindness and caring for
others.
It's lending a helping hand.

Love doesn't envy anyone else,
It's humble and courteous too.
Love is unselfish and open-
minded.
It proves that a heart is true.

Thank you, God, for instilling
your love
Into the heart of my mother,

Thelma Edwards

And thank you, God, for sending
your Son
Who taught us to love one
another.

A Student

I am a child of the living God.
From His heart He created me,
And gave me life with His own
breath,
An example of Him to be.

I exist because of His love.
He has a great purpose for me,
And as I study His "Holy Word,"
He unfolds it gradually.

Every day He teaches me more.
He opens my understanding
With all of the blessings, He
pours out,
My heart just keeps on
expanding.

Christ sent the Comforter back
for me,
To lead and to guide me each day,
And it's sweet to live in His
presence,
To follow His steps all the way.

God's Highest/Our Salvation

My soul is looking for the good
In all I say or do.
I want to live a Holy life,
A life that's pure and true.

So every day I go to God
To give Him all my praise,
And every day He answers me,
"I am with you always."

I have to be obedient.
It counts for righteousness.
When Christ saved me, He sent
me out
To comfort and to bless.

Each day I read His "Holy Word."
He leads me in His way,
And in His Word, He teaches me
Just what He wants me to say.

When you can see the Christ in
me,

You'll want to know Him too.
The Spirit in me reaches out
To touch the good in you.

My Precious Baby

Little eyes that shine so bright,
Precious smile, a pure delight,
A gift from God, I think He knew
The joy I'd have when He sent
you.

Giving and Receiving

Friendship and love are gifts from
God,
That we always give away,
But we are never destitute,
He gives us more each day.

Caring

Locks of love is a gift from the
heart
Of pure unselfish care,
Giving to someone a world of
hope,
It's love beyond compare.

When you try to help someone
each day,
Blessings come back to you,
And the whole world is a better
place,
Because of what you do.

Child of Mine

I know when you are grieving.
Each inside cry I hear.
My love is everlasting,
Erasing doubt and fear.

I'm sending you a heartful
Of joy and peace of mind,
To guide you on your journey
Eternity to find.

Entering Into Rest

Lord, can I speak the simple
truth?
It needs to be made plain.
Lord, give my tongue the words to
say,
Only You can explain.

Your presence flows all around
me.
Your love is everywhere.
It's like the very air we breathe,
But I was not aware,

Until I gave my heart to You,
And knew You are God's Son,
Until I came to ask you, Lord,
Forgive the things I've done.

That's when I felt the sweetest
Peace. Peace only You can give.
Your perfect love erased my fear,
And I began to live.

Every time I had a doubt,
I asked you what to do.
I surely had a lot of them,
But knew you'd see me through.
Thank you, Jesus.

You have got to read the Good
Book,
My grandma used to say.
All the answers still are in there,
Just talk to God. Just pray.

So I decided I would read
All of the words in red.
I would sit on the mountain side,
And listen to what He said.

Somehow the more I ask of Him,
His words come back to me,
Answering every need I have,
His Spirit keeps me free.

I rest in Jesus, praise His Name.
I know He's in control.
No matter what happens to me,
My savior guards my soul.

To Mother (who missed church today)

Judah is praising.
The Spirit is blazing.
I miss you today.
I send you His love.

Jesus has risen.
God gave us the vision.
His Son is the only way
To heaven above.

Memories

Childhood Christmases come to
mind.
My heart remembers them all.
Mother made sure that we'd have
joy,
And a Christmas tree so tall.

We had good food, such warmth,
and love,
And surely had each other.
We celebrated God's own Son,
Taught by our Christian mother.

Be Patient

The patience of God is Holy.
It's because He loves us so,
And He would have us use it,
To help our Spirits' grow.

Anger and frustration always
Make us feel sad and depressed.
But when we pray for each other,
God's love comes through, and
we're blessed.

Birthday Blessings from Jesus

Happy Birthday, child of mine.
I watch you every day.
I see you laugh. I see you smile.
I hear you when you pray.

I know when you are grieving.
I see you when you cry.
No matter what each day brings,
I'm always standing by.

The Watts Story (in honor of Dr. Martin Luther King)

"Twenty four dead," the headlines
read,
Reporting the bitter strife,
While rioting crowds fought with
police,
Whose hatred took life after life.

Rampant prejudice came to a
head,
Erupting with satanic force.
Bigoted humans acted like brutes
With no sense of wrong or
remorse.

All of the while homes were still
burning
And black, rolling smoke filled the
air,
But now the whole wide world
was watching
The sad events happening there.

Violence and looting ruled the
day.
Unspeakable fear ruled the night.
God fearing people prayed to the
Lord,
"Give us freedom. Make it right."

A spotlight was turned upon the
truth.
Viewers had watched it all.
Even those who were guilty by
just standing by
Doing nothing, were appalled.

Out of the chaos, God sent one
man
To teach nonviolence and love.
"Passive resistance is the way,"
he said,
"Ordered by God above."

Forgiveness was the message he
taught.
They killed him to stop his power.
By making a martyr out of him,
He became a lighthouse tower.

The world was stunned and
grieved at his loss.

His message will never grow old.
The same message was brought
by God's Son
And it will forever be told.
"Crucify, crucify," the maddened
crowd cried,
"Kill him. Don't let him live."
And then the crucified King of
Kings
Whispered, "Father, forgive."

Reaching out

I meet the sweetest people
In such unexpected places,
And feel the love and caring
In many friendly faces.

In fellowship with others,
God fills my heart with love.
There's something about sharing
That comes from heaven above.

And everybody that I meet
Enriches me somehow.
God lets us help each other
To meet our Savior now.

Perfect Love

Angels came and sang for joy
The night that Christ was born.
Shepherds watched with
trembling awe
Celestial praise that morn.

God had sent His only Son
To be our sacrifice,
Once for all, to save mankind.
The blood that would suffice.

Oh, the greatest love of all,
He gave for even me.
My soul will thank and praise
Him
Throughout eternity.

Survival

We all perform on the stage of life,
Showing others what we want
them to see,
Carefully guarding our vulnerable
selves
While displaying an outward
ease.

Some use bravado and blistering
pride
To convince a world that they've
defied,
And some retreat to a quiet place
To observe from the safety inside.

But all of us feel the Spirit of
God,
Who is seeking to make us His
own,
And sooner or later we have to
choose
To accept Christ or just be alone.

Thelma Edwards

When we accept Jesus, protecting
love
Surrounds us, erasing our fear,
But we meet others still guarding
their hearts,
Not knowing that Christ is here.

The Glance and the Gift

God from heaven looked down at
mankind,
And saw all the evil that day,
And said, "I have loved them from
the start,
And yet they have all turned away

"They have turned away from my
presence,
They don't even know what they
lack."
Then Jesus said, "Father, I'll go
down.
I'll redeem them and bring them
back."

The agony He bore on the cross
Was the punishment meant for
me.
He paid the price for sins I'd
done.
He redeemed me and set me free.

Thelma Edwards

Now when my Father looks down
on me,
He looks through the blood of His
Son.
The blood of my Savior covers me,
And the Holy Spirit has won.

No Regrets

Tonight, if I could turn back time,
Retrace the way I came,
I'd hold again the hand of God,
And live it just the same.

My heart has known its'
happiness,
My soul its' lonely fears,
But I have never been alone,
Forsaken and left in tears.

His presence stays beside me
To comfort and to guide.
There is no task I cannot do
With Jesus at my side.

The Mystery of God

God's answer to sin was spiritual
death,
Even though He'd given us life
and breath,
But He loved us so much, He
came and died.
Once again, we can walk by His
side.

Because Christ arose, now I can
rise.
Because He arose, I can survive.
He died for you, and He died for
me,
And He gave us back eternity.

Time/Eternity

Enjoy the gift of each new day,
To laugh and live and love.
Give thanks for blessings sent out
way,
From God in heaven above.

For time will pass us unaware
If we don't give it our best.
Don't waste a minute. Share
Christ's love,
And He will do the rest.

God Knows Our Every Thought

I thought
If I could lay old memories down
That shout so loud that they
resound
In the stillness of the night
Until sleep comes with morning
light
Then I could have the gift of
peace,
And all regrets would have to
cease.

I thought
If I could take the smallest
thought
That links to others till it's caught
In flowing images long past
Of hopes and dreams that did not
last,
Then I would put the thought
away,

And trust in God for each new
day.
The only place to go
I turned to Christ. It was not in
vain.
He took away my grief and pain.
When I bowed down my soul to
Him,
With peace He filled me to the
brim.
He took my thoughts and gave
sweet sleep,
And sent His angels, watch to
keep.

God's forgiving love
So if you think back on your life
And memories are filled with
strife,
Or joy and sadness mixed with
pain
Make you want to live it again,
Talk to Jesus; He'll make it right,
And you can sleep again at night.

What Would Jesus Say?

The words you speak can be so
sweet
To someone in despair.
So show the love Christ gave to
you
And tell someone you care.

For just a little compassion
Can heal a lot of pain,
And we are God's ambassadors.
There are souls to lose or gain.

God's Time

I have to be patient.
Although it is spring,
The weather is chilly.
I can't plant a thing.

My flower beds are ready
For all kinds of seeds,
And earth is still waiting
For the warmth it needs.

But God has His timing.
His plan includes rest.
Give thanks for His wisdom,
He knows what is best.

Grandma's House

Grandma's house had a fragrance
That was all its' very own.
The welcome there was so sweet,
I knew that I had come home.

Love permeated the room
The minute I stepped inside.
I sensed a perfect haven
For my lonely heart to hide.

A quietness enveloped
Everyone who entered there,
As if time had almost stopped
With comfort and peace to share.

Grandma had a worn Bible
With loved ones' names written
down,
And every night she'd read it
When we all would gather 'round.

Listening in the lamplight
As she read God's "Holy Word,"

I thought it was the sweetest
voice
That I had ever heard.

Kneeling down beside my chair
I heard my grandma's prayer.
She asked the Lord to bless each
one,
And keep us in His care.

Somehow I knew that Grandma's
house
Was filled with God's own love.
Living in her tender heart,
It was sent from heaven above.

That's why it was so special,
It's why I loved it so.
The house that Grandma lived in
Was the only place to go.

And all because of Grandma,
Who taught me when I was small,
I learned to trust in Jesus,
My Savior, my all in all.

His Fellowship

A visit to my sister's church
Is just like coming home,
To folks I've known and loved for
years.
They are my very own.

We are in kinship with Jesus.
We are His family.
How precious is the love of God.
How great His majesty.

Safe in Christ

The "Hope of Heaven," is the
cause
Of all the wars today.
Nations serving different "gods,"
Believe theirs' the only way.

Terrorists bring global fear,
Claim theirs' is a "Holy War,"
And in their angry, bitter zeal,
They martyr themselves the more.

But God foretold it all to us
By prophets through the ages,
And we should not be so
surprised
As Satan vents his rages.

He knows his time is almost gone.
Jesus sealed his fate,
When He died on Calvary's cross,
And opened "Heaven's Gate."

A Real Friend

You're one of those people
It's so nice to know.
You radiate sunshine
Wherever you go.

No matter what kind of
A mood that I'm in
You lift up my spirit
Again and again.

No wonder I love
The quick smile that you share.
God sometimes sends angels
Who show that they care.

Mother

In the midst of a trial
A mother will smile.
She takes time to listen
When she sees a tear glisten,
And when things go wrong
She knows many a song.
Be patient she warns.
Most roses have thorns.

Her sunshine of humor
Will brighten your day,
And chase all your rainclouds
Of gloom away.
I'm thankful that God
Gave me such a mother
Who taught all her children
To love one another.

A Precious Commission

Every day is Mother's Day
For mothers everywhere.
To lead each child to Jesus
Is every mother's prayer.

We teach our children patience.
We teach them to be kind.
We praise their generosity
And humble state of mind.

Courtesy is the gift of love
That we can demonstrate
Before our children every day,
Before it is too late.

For little hearts will listen
To what we have to say,
When we live it out for them,
And show a better way.

Politeness is so easy

When they are watching us.
Children learn unselfishness,
And share without a fuss.

We try to teach "good temper,"
It's love that will forgive.
Ill temper wounds our spirits,
It's not God's way to live.

Don't think evil of your friends.
Suspicion hurts your heart.
Just rejoice in perfect truth,
That's where God's love will start.

Then when they have grown older
With children of their own,
God brings a sweet remembrance
How parents' love is shown.

They follow in our footsteps
Each and every day,
Adopting all our values,
Mothers have to pray.

Outreach

God has given to our pastor
A vision so tremendous,
That like a windswept raging fire,
It touched our congregation,

Instilling deep within each heart
The need to reach the lost,
In our city and our nation
Regardless of the cost.

New excitement is exploding
With a sense of urgency,
To lift the name of Jesus high
From now to eternity.

We love our Savior and we'll do
Every work He gives us.
Our faith increases day by day.
We're glad that He can use us.

Wonderful things are happening
In the presence of the Lord.
There is a "Holy Harmony,"

Since we're all on one accord.

We worship and we praise his
name.
We work to give Him pleasure,
And God keeps pouring out His
love,
And blessings without measure.

Pit Stop

My son went into "Lowe's" today.
I did not know how long he'd
stay.
He said that he would be right
out,
But I confess, I had my doubt.

Grown up boys love tools as
much,
As little boys love "Toys R Us."
I prepared to wait a while,
Knowing life, I had to smile.

Sitting in his sun warmed truck,
I was surprised at my good luck,
When something jarred the old
truck bed,
And he'd come back, just like he
said.

Cancer (a Talk with God)

I'm sitting in this waiting room.
You're watching from above.
This grandchild that you gave to
me
Needs all your awesome love.

I pray you'll lead her closer, Lord.
Your Spirit is so pure.
Ease her pain and comfort her.
You are the only cure.

She doesn't know the joy and
peace,
That only you can give.
I pray she'll find the real you,
Lord,
To know your heart and live.

I'm wholly trusting you today.
I know you're in control.
Satan thinks my faith is small.
He tries to steal her soul.

You are the Savior of the world.
There's nothing he can do.
You are the "Breath of Eternity."
He knows that he is through.

We Are His Children

God is in the business
Of caring for His own.
He puts His arms around us.
We never are alone.

No matter what the circumstance,
His Spirit guides our way,
Filling us with joy and peace,
And faith to face each day.

Gray Head Counsel

A lot of years have passed us by.
We've done a lot of living.
We've weathered storms along the
way,
And still our hearts keep giving.

Our children need our sound
advice,
And a sturdy helping hand.
We've learned from all our own
mistakes,
Not to build on shifting sand.

But each new crop of young
adults
Will choose what they think is
best.
Some will respect by listening,
And let their lives be blessed.

We point them to the "Word of
God"
And what He has to say.

He left his counsel there for us,
Our guide for every day.

To a Perfect Stranger (on a rainy day in April)

He had a wonderful mother.
I know this to be true.
He wiped his feet on the door
mat,
As he was coming through.

Seldom there are customers
That give that much respect
To a caring type of business
They know, but just neglect.

I feel a sense of gratitude.
I'm one who taught my own.
Thank God for his loving mother.
I know I'm not alone.

Time to Take Cover (tornado watch)

What an adventure.
The sirens are blowing.
I'm down in the basement
Just waiting -- not knowing.

A storm is heading
Directly toward us,
But we are prepared.
We have candles and such.

I haven't heard wind
Or any raindrops yet.
We'll be glad when it's over,
Even our pet.

She flew down the stairsteps.
She is a smart cat.
When I saw her run down,
I said, "Well, that is that."
Time to take cover!

Thelma Edwards

Our Pastor -- Recognition

How can we find the words to say
How much you're appreciated?
We know God has anointed you
In the life you've dedicated.

God uses his gifted people
To show us that Jesus is real.
The presence of peace around you
Is a sense of joy we can feel.

Your love, Oh God, flows out to
us
To lead and to guide us each day.
Bless the shepherd you have
sent,
With the words you'd have him
say,

And bless us too, to do your will,
And to share your redeeming
love.

Let your Spirit reach out through
us,
To show them your Heaven
above.

Jesus Has the Answers

Jesus my Savior came to me,
And asked me if I would like to be
free.
Free from my lonely grief and
pain.
He said He would fill me with joy
again

"Have mercy, Lord," was my
earnest prayer,
With forgiving love, He met me
there,
Filling my soul with perfect peace,
Vanquishing fear with a sweet
release,
And now His Spirit guides my
way,
His presence protects me every
day.

Our Church Family

When I come through the door of
my church,
God's presence flows out to meet
me,
And I see a smile in every eye
Of those who are there to greet
me.

I have to pray and thank my God
For bringing me to this place.
The wonder and joy of His Spirit
Is glowing on every face.

I am so glad that I know Jesus.
He answers my every prayer.
Whatever happens in my life
I don't worry. I know He's there.

When I see folks who are
searching,
And don't know what they're
searching for,
I tell them all about Jesus

About heaven, and how He is the
Door.

Whoever comes to Him, He saves,
And He loves them and sets them
free,
Free of heartache and free of
pain,
Free to be in His family.

Fellowship with the Savior
Is a foretaste of "Heaven's Glory."
What a promise He gives to us
When we study the Bible story.

Time

The air is crisp, fresh and cool.
There is a welcome breeze.
Autumn has arrived again.
I watch the falling leaves,

Whirling, floating, drifting down,
Finishing their season.
And I thank God for my life.
I'm here for a reason.

The Quest

Who am I in the sight of God?
What am I doing on the path I
trod?
When will I understand it all?
My God always answers when I
call.

Sweet Peace

I've come home to Jesus.
I see Him, "Face to face."
Joy beyond description
Is now in my embrace.

I hear angels singing
A love song to the Lamb.
Holy, Holy praises,
He is the great "I am."

I am in His presence.
His Spirit is my own.
I am with my Savior,
So glad that I've come home.

Thank You, God, for Angels

There is a restless searching
When you haven't yet met God.
Everything seems out of place,
And really, sort of odd.

You don't know why you're lonely
And sometimes feeling blue.
You wish there were an answer
But don't know what to do.

Nothing seems to satisfy
No matter what you try.
You play a part for others,
And think you're getting by.

Then everything gets harder,
You wonder, "What's the use?"
"This world holds nothing for me
But trouble and abuse."

When all of life seems empty
With nothing but despair,
God always sends an angel,

And he will meet you there,

At your point of giving up,
Your pain too much to bear.
God can fill your heart with joy.
He saves and answers prayer.

50th Anniversary

Do you remember the day we
met?
My heart was so full, I can't
forget.
I wondered if God was showing
me
A vision of what my life could be?

We learned to love and trust each
other,
And had no need to seek another.
If days were sunny or cloudy or
gray,
Thank God we always knew how
to pray.

Trials and tests made us give a
sigh,
Not knowing whether to laugh or
cry.
Sometimes we didn't know what
to do,

And agonized, but God saw us
through.

When our children came, our
home was filled
With the sweetest blessings He
had willed.
Love and laughter were part of
each day.
Visitors came and wished they
could stay.

The warmth of our home, with
love to share,
Drew like a magnet everyone
there,
And now, looking back across the
years,
We've weathered it all, the joy, the
tears.

I wondered then; God was
showing me
The vision of what my life would
be.
Do you remember that day we
met?
I love you still, I'll never forget.

From a Child's Point of View (Father's Day)

Mom said,
"Go tell Dad; he'll know what to
do."
So, I'll tell Dad what I'm going
through.
Dad is smart. He'll straighten it
out.
My dad knows what it's all about.

When problems come, I talk to
Dad.
He's the best friend I've ever had.
Dad trusts in God, I heard him
pray,
"Lord, let me teach my son,
today."

Dad is loved for so many things,
Mostly the courage that he
brings.
Sharing the love of God with all,
Look at Dad. He's standing tall.

Love Passed On

A heart that's filled
With love and care,
Will always find
A way to share.

The little things
Life has to give
That makes it easier
To live.

The friends we meet
Along the way
Are sent by God
To bless each day,

And when we share
A smile or song,
It helps to pass
The day along.

Raw loneliness
Besets us all
Until we heed

Thelma Edwards

Our Savior's call,

And each of us
Seeks peace of mind
That only God
Can let us find.

Friendship is a
Holy part of
Letting God touch
Another's heart.

God Silently Speaks

From my open bedroom window
In the gray of dawn's first light,
I breathe the freshest, cool, clean
air,
After childlike sleep last night.

My soul in wonder feels your love
With an inner, wordless praise.
Thank you, God, for reminding
me,
I can come to you always.

As the day unfolds its' promise,
There are choices I must make.
Lord, let my life be true to you.
Order each step that I take.

Help me to meet someone today,
Who needs your redeeming love.
Give me words I need to say.
Touch them with peace from
above.

Daddy (on your 58th birthday)

If we could only let you know,
And live our lives so true,
With honesty and integrity,
In all, we say and do,

To justify the love you gave
All through our younger years,
And still, you're here with helping
hand,
And still, you calm our fears.

If we could only tell you now,
We love you, and we care,
And respect the things you stand
for,
The life that's fair and square.

Never Ending Love

When your days are filled with
stress,
And everything just seems a
mess,
You don't have to carry it all
alone.
Your God still sits there on His
throne.

He waits to fill your heart with
peace.
Just call on Him for sweet
release.
With love, He'll sort it out for you.
You are His child. He'll see you
through.

Happy Birthday, I Love You (to my great grandson)

Monnie McGee is four today.
He's the smartest kid in the
U.S.A.
He bubbles with laughter, with
mischievous eyes.
Every day is a new surprise.

"Hi Grandma," he calls,
As he comes through the door.
I ask, "Where is my hug?"
And he gives me one more,

Then he races off
In a hurry to play,
Not knowing that he
Has just made my day.

Karl

You are my precious grandson,
You have a birthday today.
I miss your sense of humor,
And your quiet caring way.

God gave you a special talent,
To sketch pictures with your
heart,
That show your inner feelings,
With a message to impart.

I see the light in your eyes,
And your mischievous grin,
You always lift my spirit
No matter what mood I'm in.

What a blessing to my soul,
To know that you're in God's
care,
Trusting in His "Holy Word,"
And turning to Him in prayer.

Nurses (God's Special People)

Silently coming and going at
night,
Making sure everything still is
alright,
The comfort of knowing someone
is there
Is a gift from God, from angels
who care.

There is a kindness that comes
from the heart,
With understanding and love to
impart,
That reaches out across sadness
and pain,
And lets us thank God again and
again.

Say Hello

Laughter is a medicine
To keep us young each day.
So share a smile and after while
Your "blahs" will go away.

Say "Hello," to everyone.
It's just unspoken love.
Recognize the brotherhood
That's sent from God above.

My Family -- My Friends

I asked my God for riches
To help you find a way
To ease the heavy burdens
That you carry every day.

But, He said, "There is a purpose
For every joy and pain."
He said to ask Him for the
answers.
Every loss is for a gain,

And since I gave my heart to him,
He guards my soul each day.
All I have to do is trust Him,
He always leads the way.

I love you all so dearly,
But God loves you much, much
more,
And He has all the answers,
That you are looking for.

My Precious Daughter

Before you were born, God
Answered my prayer,
That He would surround you
With loving care.

No matter what tests
This life would bring,
I asked Him to give you
A song to sing,

And when you asked Jesus
To fill your soul,
He lovingly entered
And made you whole.

There were times when life
Offered tears and pain,
But you sought the Lord,
Again and again.

No matter what problems
That came to you,
You knew that He always
Would see you through.

Our God has been with you
Down through the years,
Leading and guiding you,
Calming your fears.

The gift He gave you,
Compassion and prayer,
Is a witness true
Of His love and care.

When I glorify
My Savior's name,
He reminds me of
The day you came.

Devotion

Marriage is a mental picture
Of the Holy love of God,
Two souls promising their lives
To the path that Jesus trod.

It is a sacred unity,
God's Spirit joined with our own,
A witness of salvation
With joy we've never known.

With an oath to God, we promise
To cherish and love one another,
To protect and give respect
All of our lives to each other,

And in the shelter of His care,
Our home will be a haven of rest.
He watches all our hopes and
dreams,
And we know that we are blessed.

It's a wondrous privilege
Just to call on Him in prayer,

To worship and to praise His
name,
Just knowing that He is there.

We're starting our life together.
"Lord, let our lives be a praise.
Use us Lord, in your Holy will,
And keep us Lord, all of our
days."

When You Don't Know God, Nor Care

If I were God, would I forgive
The sinful things you do?
The words you speak can cause
such pain
For others to go through,

Or would I cause your heart to
change,
With overflowing love,
With peace and joy and Holiness,
From Father up above?

Since Jesus saved my searching
soul,
He's made it plain to me.
I can share His precious love.
He wants to set you free.

This world is filled with ugliness,
With sorrow and with tears,
But Christ can give you perfect
peace.
Just talk to Him. He hears.

The Reason

Pain like knives, cutting
Into my chest,
Cruel hot pain, stabbing
Into my breast.

Wave after wave,
Enveloping me,
Taking all of my breath
Away from me,

Connected coughs 'til
My breath is gone,
Then catching it back
Like a child, new born.

Those precious seconds
That I can breathe,
I thank God for
His mercy received.

I think of the price
Christ paid for me,
As He bled and died

In agony.

No pain on earth could
Ever compare
To the pain my Savior
Suffered there.

My heart knows I must
Sometimes feel pain,
Just to remind me
Of His again.

To My Hospital Neighbor

Yesterday

I heard you cry out
To God today,
In swift sharp pain, and
I had to pray.

"Lord, heal her body,
Release her pain,
Restore her to health
With strength again.

Comfort her Father
With Holy peace,
And let any fears
Totally cease."

Destiny

This day is part of
Eternity.
The choices I make
Are up to me.

Hungry for spiritual
Food each day,
I turn to You, Jesus,
Guide my way.

Since you saved me,
My life has grown sweet,
Sharing your love
With people I meet.

They always listen,
Eager to know,
How to find peace
In this world below.

You pour out blessings
Day after day.
I have to thank you.

I have to pray.

When time has brought me
Before your throne,
I'll stand before you,
And you alone.

God Hears Us and Answers

What a blessing to be back
In the "House of God" today,
With my precious family,
Thankful you knew how to pray.

Lord, you listen every time,
And take away my fear.
What a sacred privilege
Just to know that you are here.